Contents

KT-115-969

Some words are printed in bold, **like this**. You can find out what they mean on page 30. You can also look in the box at the bottom of the page where they first appear.

With no warning

It was a summer day more than 1,200 years ago. All was quiet on an island off the north of England. The island was called Lindisfarne. (See map on page 9.) Holy men called **monks** lived on this island. They lived in a church full of treasure.

Suddenly **longships** swept to the shore. Longships were fast boats owned by Vikings. Men in helmets jumped from the boats. Their swords were drawn. The monks had no idea who their attackers were. Some monks ran away.

longship fast Viking boat
monk holy Christian man
slave someone who is bought and sold to work without pay

ON TO VALHALLA!

Tristan Boyer Binns

www.raintreepublishers.co.uk
Visit our website to find out more information about **Raintree** books.

To order:
☎ Phone 44 (0) 1865 888112
📄 Send a fax to 44 (0) 1865 314091
💻 Visit the Raintree bookshop at **www.raintreepublishers.co.uk** to browse our catalogue and order online.

First published in Great Britain by Raintree,
Halley Court, Jordan Hill, Oxford OX2 8EJ,
part of Harcourt Education.

Raintree is a registered trademark of Harcourt
Education Ltd.

© Harcourt Education Ltd 2008
First published in paperback in 2008
The moral right of the proprietor has been asserted.

All rights reserved. No part of this publication may be
reproduced, stored in a retrieval system, or transmitted
in any form or by any means, electronic, mechanical,
photocopying, recording, or otherwise, without either
the prior written permission of the publishers or a
licence permitting restricted copying in the United
Kingdom issued by the Copyright Licensing Agency
Ltd, 90 Tottenham Court Road, London W1T 4LP
(www.cla.co.uk).

Editorial: Louise Galpine and Claire Throp
Design: Richard Parker and Tinstar Design
         www.tinstar.co.uk
Illustrations: Steve Weston, International Mapping
Picture research: Mica Brancic
Production: Julie Carter

Originated by Modern Age
Printed and bound in China by Leo Paper Group

ISBN 978 1 4062 0768 2 (hardback)
12 11 10 09 08
10 9 8 7 6 5 4 3 2 1

ISBN 978 1 4062 0775 0 (paperback)
12 11 10 09 08
10 9 8 7 6 5 4 3 2 1

British Library Cataloguing in Publication Data
Boyer Binns, Tristan
On to Valhalla!. – (Fusion)
293
A full catalogue record for this book is available from
the British Library

Acknowledgements
The publishers would like to thank the following
for permission to reproduce photographs: The Art
Archive/Richard Wagner Museum Bayreuth/Dagli
Orti (A) p. **15**; The Trustees of the British Museum
p. **25**; Corbis pp. **7** (Ted Spiegel), **14** (Charles &
Josette Lenars), **18** (Richard T. Nowitz), **23** (Carmen
Redondo), **24** (Chris Lisle), **28** (Nik Wheeler); Corbis/
Bettmann p. **10–11**; DK Images p.**12** (Andy Crawford);
Werner Forman Archive pp. **17** main pic, **27**, **29**
(Statens Historiska Museum, Stockholm), **17** inset pic
(Thjodminjasafn, Reykjavik, Iceland).

Cover photograph of Oseberg replica Viking ship,
Norway, reproduced with permission of Getty Images/
Robert Harding World Imagery/David Lomax.

Every effort has been made to contact copyright
holders of any material reproduced in this book. Any
omissions will be rectified in subsequent printings if
notice is given to the publishers.

The publishers would like to thank Nancy Harris and
Richard Hall for their assistance with the preparation of
this book.

Disclaimer
All the Internet addresses (URLs) given in this book
were valid at the time of going to press. However, due
to the dynamic nature of the Internet, some addresses
may have changed, or sites may have changed or
ceased to exist since publication. While the author and
publishers regret any inconvenience this may cause
readers, no responsibility for any such changes can be
accepted by either the author or the publishers.

It is recommended that adults supervise children on
the Internet.

The attackers took other monks to sell as **slaves**. Slaves were unpaid workers. They took treasures from the church. Then they set sail for home.

Viking fact!

Longships could go in shallow or deep water. They were good to take on oceans and rivers. Dragons were sometimes carved on the front. They looked scary!

The attack at Lindisfarne was over quickly. This was the first sign of a scary new force.

From the sea

Viking **raiders** made surprise attacks on people. They came from the countries of Denmark, Norway, and Sweden (see map on page 9).

Vikings loved to fight and sail. Viking boys learned to be **warriors** (fighters) and sailors.

Viking raids brought them glory. Raiding also brought riches. The Vikings held great feasts back at home. Poets (writers) told long stories about their brave battles.

Some Viking raiders were full-time warriors. But most were also farmers. When there was little farm work the men set sail. Their wives and children stayed home. They looked after the farm.

After a raid the Vikings sold the treasure. They also sold the **slaves** they took. The raiders shared the money they made.

Viking fact!

Vikings were not afraid to die. They believed that if you died in battle you went straight to Viking heaven.

raider someone who makes surprise attacks
warrior person who is trained to fight and do battle

This is a gravestone at Lindisfarne. It shows the solid wall of Viking raiders that the monks faced.

The Viking Age

Vikings were very **loyal** to their leaders. This meant they followed their leaders into battle whatever happened. The leader was called a **chieftain**. A group of chieftains were loyal to a king. They followed their king into wars.

There was not enough good farmland for all the Vikings. Many Vikings went to war to win land. They settled in new places far from home.

Other Vikings loved to sail off and explore new lands. They wanted to find new places to live and get rich. Some found places where no one lived yet. Iceland and Greenland were cold, and full of ice and snow.

Some Vikings became traders. They bought and sold **goods** from all over the world. They bought goods such as silver and pottery. They sold goods such as honey and wool.

chieftain powerful local leader
goods things of value
loyal sticking to someone whatever happens

Viking fact!

Iceland – the name tells you how much ice there is! But there are also good places to farm. Vikings first settled there more than 1,000 years ago.

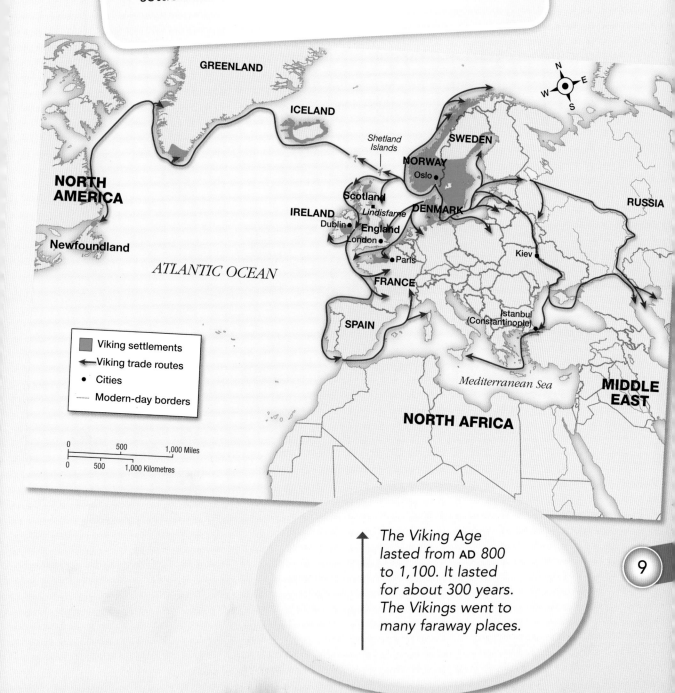

GREENLAND

ICELAND

Shetland Islands

SWEDEN

NORWAY
Oslo

NORTH AMERICA

Scotland
Lindisfarne

DENMARK

RUSSIA

IRELAND
Dublin
London
England

Kiev

Newfoundland

ATLANTIC OCEAN

Paris

FRANCE

Istanbul (Constantinople)

SPAIN

Mediterranean Sea

MIDDLE EAST

NORTH AFRICA

- ▪ Viking settlements
- ← Viking trade routes
- • Cities
- --- Modern-day borders

| 0 | 500 | 1,000 Miles |
| 0 | 500 | 1,000 Kilometres |

The Viking Age lasted from AD 800 to 1,100. It lasted for about 300 years. The Vikings went to many faraway places.

Sword and shield

Vikings did not wear uniforms when raiding. Each **warrior** looked different, but all were scary!

Shields were made of wooden planks. They were shaped into a circle. An iron grip in the middle kept the warrior's hand safe. They were strong and heavy. They could bash down enemies.

Viking fact!

Swords were made from metal twisted together. The twisted metal was hammered flat. Then the edges were made very sharp.

armour layers of tough clothes to keep the wearer safe

The more money a Viking had, the better he could protect himself. The best **armour** was made from metal. It also cost the most. Metal links were hammered together to make shirts. They were called chain mail shirts. They were hard to cut through with a sword. The poorer warriors had leather shirts and helmets.

*Vikings sailed in **longships** on raids. They waited in long rows for the attack.*

Raiding away!

Vikings attacked targets all over Europe. Viking **raiders** could sail their **longships** up rivers. They reached cities far from the coast this way. They even raided Paris, France (see map on page 13).

The French king was very scared of the Vikings. He paid them money to stay away. Other rulers (leaders) paid too. In England this money was known as **Danegeld**. Sometimes rulers paid so much the country had no money left. But the Vikings just attacked again.

Viking helmets never had horns. Some artists and film-makers decided they looked too plain. They added horns to make them look scarier!

berserker Viking warrior who thought nothing could hurt him
Danegeld money paid to keep Vikings away
frenzy being wildly excited or crazy for a short time

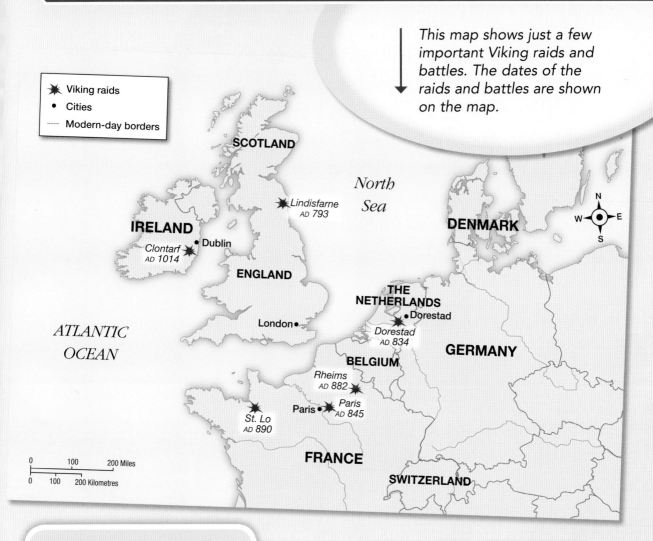

This map shows just a few important Viking raids and battles. The dates of the raids and battles are shown on the map.

Key:
- ✸ Viking raids
- • Cities
- --- Modern-day borders

SCOTLAND

North Sea

IRELAND

Lindisfarne AD 793

DENMARK

Clontarf AD 1014 • Dublin

ENGLAND

THE NETHERLANDS

• Dorestad

Dorestad AD 834

ATLANTIC OCEAN

London •

GERMANY

BELGIUM

Rheims AD 882

Paris • Paris AD 845

St. Lo AD 890

FRANCE

SWITZERLAND

0   100   200 Miles
0   100   200 Kilometres

N W E S

Going berserk

There were some Viking **warriors** even scarier than the rest. They were called **berserkers**. A **frenzy** took over them. It is said that they bit their shields. They also ground their teeth. They ran into battle without **armour**. Berserkers thought nothing could harm them.

13

Valhalla

Even the fearless Vikings died in battle. But this was not a bad thing. Vikings believed that they went to a perfect place, like heaven. This was known as an **afterlife**. For Vikings **Valhalla** was their afterlife. In Valhalla the **warriors** did battle all day. At night their wounds healed. They held a non-stop party all night long. At dawn they began fighting again.

Vikings drew pictures of Valkyries. Valkyries took dead warriors to Valhalla. Valhalla is the hall with the curved roof.

14

afterlife place where Vikings went when they died
Valhalla hall where dead warriors battled and feasted
Valkyries warrior maidens who flew to Viking battles

Viking fact!

Were there any
real Viking women
warriors? Some
pictures show women
with spears. There are
stories of women on
raids. Some Viking
women are said to
have led armies.

← Artists still love to
make pictures of
Valkyries taking
brave dead warriors
to Valhalla.

Vikings believed in **Valkyries**. Valkyries were flying warrior
women. They watched over battles on Earth. They decided
who would live and who would die. Then Valkyries scooped
up the fallen warriors. They flew them to Valhalla.

Viking gods

The Vikings believed in many gods and goddesses. Each one helped with something special. The Viking gods lived in a place called **Asgard**. **Valhalla** was the place where dead warriors went. It was in Asgard, too.

Odin	Odin was the most important god. He was wise and powerful. Odin sat at the head of the feasts in Valhalla.
Frigg	Frigg was Odin's wife. She was the goddess of good health and beauty.
Thor	Thor was very strong. But he was not very bright. He had a hammer. When he swung it, lightning flashed. When the hammer hit things, thunder boomed.
Frey	Frey blessed people with children. He blessed farmers with good crops (for example, corn). He had a twin sister called Freya. She was the goddess of love and death.
Loki	Loki was clever and dishonest. He was Odin's brother. He liked playing mean tricks.

Viking fact!

Some of the names we still use for days of the week come from Viking times. Thursday is Thor's day. Wednesday is Odin's day. Friday is named after Freya or Frigg. No one is sure which!

This is the god called Thor. He was very powerful.

Freya was the goddess of love. She later became the goddess of war and death.

17

Why in a boat?

Many brave Viking **warriors** died in battle. Many were buried where they died. Some were brought home for **funerals**. A great **chieftain** or king had an amazing funeral.

What was the best way to be buried? In a fine **longship**, of course. Viking boats meant speed and adventure. A funeral boat sped to the **afterlife**.

This burial boat was found in Gokstad, Norway. The boat is beautifully made. The man buried in it was very rich. He had three other smaller boats in the burial mound as well!

18

This is a photo of a bridle mount. A bridle mount is a buckle. It was part of the headgear used to control a horse.

The boat was not enough. The dead chieftain needed the same things he used when he was alive. He was dressed in his finest clothes. He had his weapons and jewellery. His funeral boat was filled with food. It also had servants and animals. Then the whole funeral boat was buried in a big mound.

Quick trip to paradise

Vikings wanted to get to the **afterlife** (heaven) quickly. They believed they could get there faster travelling in a burning boat. A traveller called Ibn Fadlan saw a Viking **chieftain's funeral**. It was in Russia. He wrote about what he saw.

This is what a Viking funeral might have looked like.

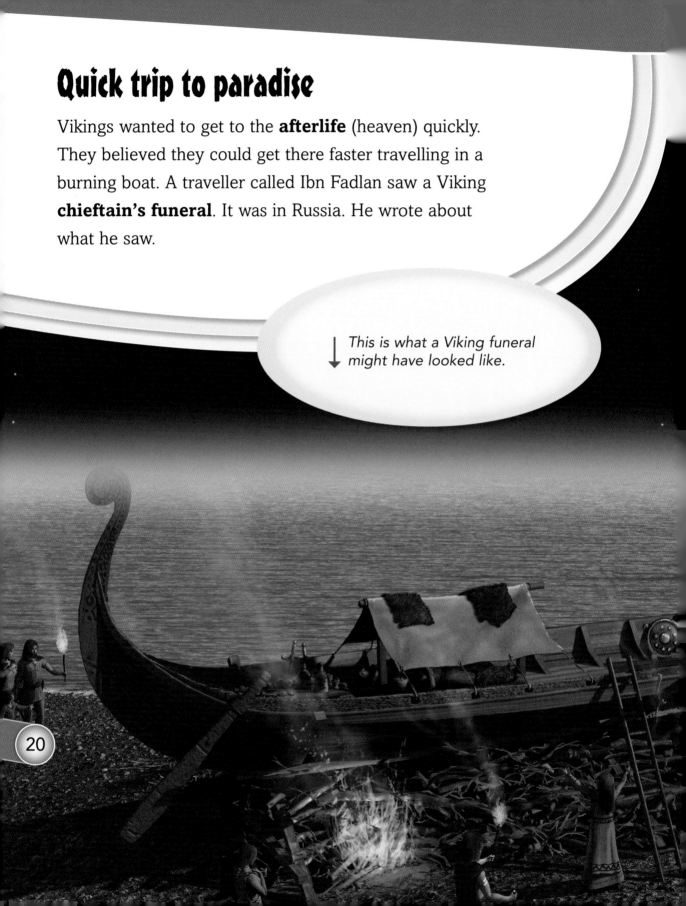

What Ibn Fadlan saw...

- A **slave** girl offered to be killed. She would be buried along with her master.

- People dressed the dead chieftain in fine robes. They laid him out on the ship. They put in weapons and food. Next they added a musical instrument and animals.

- The slave girl was given a drink that stopped her feeling pain. Then she was brought to the ship. An old woman strangled her.

- The chieftain's closest relative walked backwards to the ship. He set it on fire. Then all the other people brought flaming sticks to the fire.

- In less than an hour the whole ship had burned. So had everything in it. The people said the souls had gone quickly to the afterlife.

Sagas and runes

The Vikings remembered their leaders and heroes. They had poets (writers). The poets made up long stories about their bravery. They were told out loud at feasts. Friends, family, and special guests listened to the stories.

The Vikings did not have an easy written language. They used marks called **runes**. They had no curves in them. Runes were carved into wood and stone. Runes were not good for writing down long stories.

Hundreds of years later other people wrote down some of these stories. They used letters instead of runes. These stories are called **sagas**. They tell us about famous people. They tell us about the things they did.

Viking fact!

One famous saga from Iceland tells about a raid. It gives a clear and scary picture of what a Viking raid was like.
"I've been with sword and spear slippery with bright blood ... raging we killed and killed."

runes Viking alphabet marks made up of short, straight lines
sagas Viking stories about famous people and battles

Rune stones are all over the Viking world. There is a famous one in the country of Denmark. The runes are in the line along the bottom.

Burying others

What if you were not a **warrior**? When you died, what happened? Some Vikings were kings or queens. Others were farmers. Many were **slaves**. A few were thieves who stole other people's things. Each was buried differently.

The poor often had simple graves. They had stones placed around them in the shape of a boat.

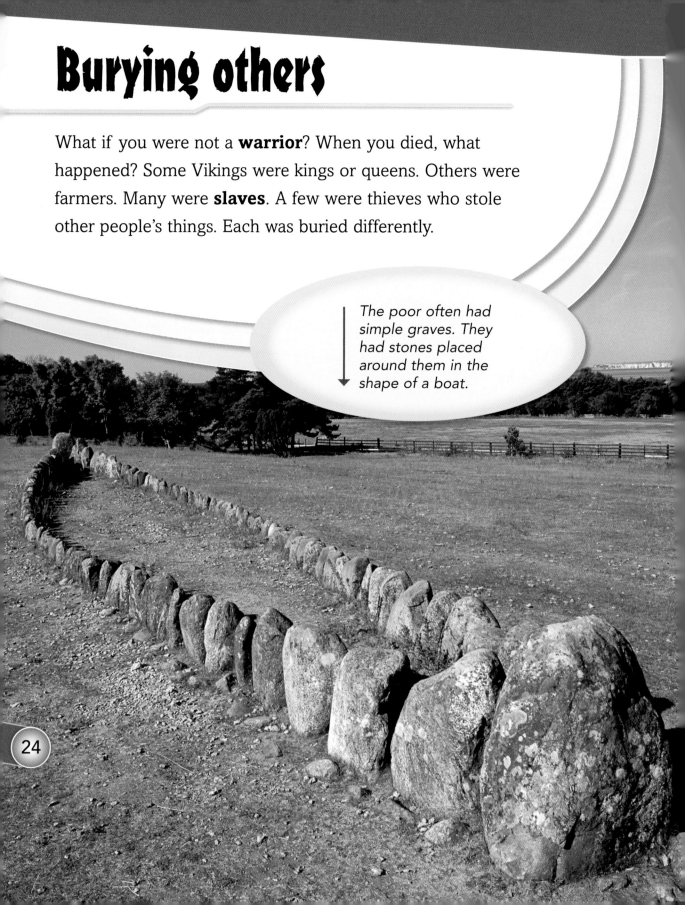

Person	How buried	With anything?
Slave	Left out as food for dogs and birds	Nothing
Thief	Hanged until dead, then left as food for dogs and birds	Nothing
Farmer or poor man	Buried or burned in a small boat. If poorer, in a mound grave surrounded by stones in the shape of a ship.	Whatever could be spared. Sometimes just one knife.
Craftsman	In a pit, maybe covered by a mound	Tools of his trade, food, beer
Woman	In a pit, maybe covered by a mound	Things from around the house, such as kitchen items, combs, food
Warrior	If rich, in a boat. If poorer, in a mound grave surrounded by stones in the shape of a ship.	Weapons, food, horse. The bravest warrior was buried in his ship.
Rich woman or queen	Placed in a fine boat or wagon. Buried in a mound or maybe burned.	Finest clothes, food, beer, jewellery, kitchen items, dogs, slaves
Rich man or king	Placed in a fine boat. Buried in a great mound or burned.	Finest clothes, food, beer, jewellery, weapons, slaves

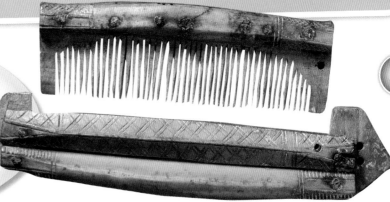

This comb and case was found in York. It is 1,000 years old and still has all its teeth!

Changes

Most of the people in Europe followed the **Christian** religion. This was based on the teachings of Jesus Christ. The Vikings started raiding Christians in Europe. They slowly became Christians, too.

Viking leaders became Christians. They started building churches. Whole Viking countries became Christian.

Viking **funerals** changed slowly, too. The Viking boat funerals grew less common. People began to be buried in Christian graveyards. Some people were still buried with special things. These were things they would need in the **afterlife** (heaven).

The Vikings were powerful for about 300 years. By 1100 all of the Vikings became Christian. That was 900 years ago. They gave up their old gods. They stopped raiding so much. They settled happily where they were. The Viking Age was over.

Viking fact!

Vikings needed to trade with Christians. They started to wear crosses. The crosses made Christians feel better about the scary Vikings.

Christian someone who follows the teachings of Jesus Christ

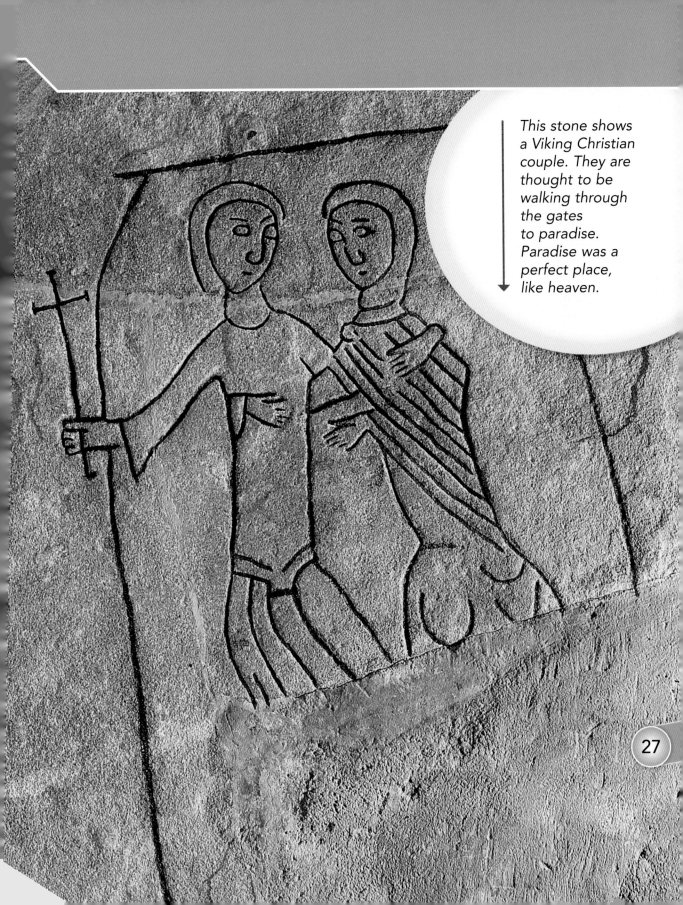

This stone shows a Viking Christian couple. They are thought to be walking through the gates to paradise. Paradise was a perfect place, like heaven.

27

Famous Vikings

Eric the Red (about 950-1003)

Eric the Red was born in Norway. His family moved to Iceland when he was ten. In 982 he was sent away from Iceland after he killed two men. He sailed off to explore. He found a cold and icy island. He called it Greenland. He took more than 400 people from Iceland to settle there. Vikings lived in Greenland until the 1400s.

Leif Ericsson (about 980-1020)

Eric the Red had three sons. Leif Ericsson was his middle son. In 1000 Leif sailed for North America. He found a place he called Vinland. He later returned to Greenland. He told others about Vinland. Leif stayed in Greenland. Leif's father died. Leif became the leader. Later a group of settlers went to live in Vinland.

This is a statue of Leif Ericsson.

Timeline

AD

793
England is shocked when Vikings attack Lindisfarne.

795
Viking terror spreads with raids on Scotland and Ireland.

835
Vikings raid England, France, and Germany.

845
After a very bloody raid on Paris, Vikings are bribed with **Danegeld** to stay away.

860
Vikings go even further in Constantinople (where Europe meets Asia), North Africa, and Italy.

862
Swedish Vikings sail down rivers to make fortunes trading in Russia.

866
Based in York, Vikings take over a huge part of England.

921
Travelling through Russia, Ibn Fadlan watches a Viking **chieftain's** burning boat **funeral**.

960s
The country of Denmark becomes **Christian**.

986
Exploring far from home, Eric the Red finds Greenland.

995
Norway is the next Viking country to become Christian.

around 1000
Iceland and Greenland become Christian.

around 1000
After a few attempts, Leif Ericsson finds North America.

1066
Finally defeated! Vikings lose a major battle in England.

around 1100
Sweden is the final Viking country to become Christian.

around 1100
The world is safe from these **raiders** as the Viking Age ends.

1200s
Viking **sagas** are first written down. Nobody knows how close they are to real events.

29

Glossary

afterlife place where Vikings went when they died. The afterlife was seen as a perfect place, like heaven.

armour layers of tough clothes to keep the wearer safe. Some Viking warriors wore armour.

Asgard home of the gods. Odin and Thor lived in Asgard.

berserker Viking warrior who thought nothing could hurt him. Berserkers scared everyone, even other Vikings!

chieftain powerful local leader. A chieftain could hope to become a king.

Christian someone who follows the teachings of Jesus Christ. Many Vikings later became Christians.

Danegeld money paid to keep Vikings away. The Danegeld did not work because they came back anyway!

frenzy being wildly excited or crazy for a short time. Beserkers were thought to go into a frenzy as they went into battle.

funeral ceremony held when someone dies. At a Viking funeral Vikings were often buried with things they had used in their lives.

goods things of value. Vikings bought and sold goods in all the countries they raided.

longship fast Viking boat. Longships were the best boats of their time.

loyal sticking to someone whatever happens. Warriors were loyal to their leaders.

monk holy Christian man. Monks were not ready to fight.

raider someone who makes surprise attacks. Raiders struck fear into their enemies all over Europe.

runes Viking alphabet marks made up of short, straight lines. Runes were easy to carve into stone.

sagas Viking stories about famous people and battles. Sagas were added to over the years.

slave someone who is bought and sold to work without pay. Slaves were often traded by the Vikings.

Valhalla hall where dead warriors battled and feasted. Valhalla was huge!

Valkyries warrior maidens who flew to Viking battles. The Valkyries hosted the battles and feasts in Valhalla.

warrior person who is trained to fight and do battle. Viking warriors were strong and scary.

Want to know more?

Books to read

History Makers: The Vikings, Jackie Gaff (Parragon, 2003)

Picture the Past: Life on a Viking Ship, Jane Shuter (Heinemann Library, 2005)

Viking, Susan M. Margeson (DK Eyewitness Books, 2005)

Websites

http://www.bbc.co.uk/schools/vikings/index.shtml
The BBC has a history site for children. The section on Vikings even has a quiz
– are you up to the challenge?

http://teacher.scholastic.com/products/instructor/vikings.htm
This online quiz has links to other websites all about the Vikings.

Read about ancient
Rome in **Staying Alive
in Ancient Rome**.

Read about ancient
Greece in **Welcome to
the Ancient Olympics!**

Index